ISLAND STYLE

ISLAND STYLE

Jim Kemp

FRIEDMAN/FAIRFAX

A FRIEDMAN/FAIRFAX BOOK

© 2002 by Michael Friedman Publishing Group, Inc.

Please visit our website: www.metrobooks.com

Library of Congress Cataloging-in-Publication Data

Kemp, Jim.
   Island style / [Jim Kemp].
     p.cm. -- (Architecture and design library)
   Includes bibliographic references and index
   ISBN 1-58663-304-X
    1. Interior decoration—United States—History—20th century. 2. Decoration and ornament—Caribbean Area—Influence. 3. Decoration and ornament—Oceania—Influence. I. Title. II. Series.

NK2004 .K46 2002
729'.0973'0904--dc21

2001050148

Editor: Hallie Einhorn
Art Director: Kevin Ullrich
Designer: Orit Mardkha-Tenzer
Photography Editor: Lori Epstein
Production Manager: Michael Vagnetti

Color separations by Colourscan
Printed in China by C S Graphics Shanghai Co., Ltd.

1 3 5 7 9 10 8 6 4 2

Distributed by Sterling Publishing Company, Inc.
387 Park Avenue South
New York, NY 10016
Distributed in Canada by Sterling Publishing
Canadian Manda Group
One Atlantic Avenue, Suite 105
Toronto, Ontario, Canada M6K 3E7
Distributed in Australia by
Capricorn Link (Australia) Pty, Ltd.
P.O. Box 704, Windsor, NSW 2756 Australia

For Jean Heidt Carter and Janet Heidt Roberts

Contents

INTRODUCTION

With the power of a tidal wave, island style is rolling toward the shores of the decorating world. Leading the way are rattan and bamboo furnishings, sisal carpeting, and palettes of bright whites and tropical pastels. These charming decorative elements are accompanied by such delightful accessories as carved wooden bowls and colorful dinnerware bedecked with island motifs.

While island style has a number of interpretations, this book focuses on decorating schemes featuring influences from the Caribbean and the South Pacific. Although these types of designs have their own distinct nuances, they also share many traits.

Island style immediately conjures up powerful images of paradise or a modern-day Eden. Whether the tone is Caribbean or Indonesian, the impact is visual and visceral. Hearing the names "Bali" and "Jamaica" immediately brings to mind clear blue seas and dazzling white sand beneath a golden sun. These enchanting locales also offer the promise of relaxation and, perhaps, a hint of high adventure waiting just beyond the horizon.

The rich images that we associate with the islands have a long history. From Paul Gauguin's nineteenth-century paintings of Tahiti to the twentieth-century musical *South Pacific*, the tropical islands of Oceania have seized and held the public's imagination.

Under less-than-ideal circumstances, servicemen in World War II's Pacific Theater experienced the charms of Oceania firsthand. And with Hawaii's admittance in 1959 as the fiftieth state, the Pacific Islands region started becoming an integral part of the fabric of Western culture and imagination.

The same can be said of the Caribbean. In the years following the Spanish-American War, people flocked to enjoy the charms of Havana. In fact, many a couple honeymooned in pre-Castro Cuba, bringing home tales of sun-soaked days and casino-filled nights, both cooled by gentle ocean breezes.

The Caribbean remains a favorite tourist destination. Puerto Rico and the Virgin Islands, both American and British, sing a siren song to

OPPOSITE: *Natural earth tones, creamy white linens, and an evocative ceiling fan unite to give this room island airs. A screen reminiscent of shutters heightens the mood while serving as a novel headboard.*

vacationers, especially during winter when warm beaches lure snow-bound northerners.

Although the islands of the Caribbean and Oceania are far from each other, they nonetheless share a similar architectural history. The first dwellings represented the vernacular architecture of these far-flung destinations. Eminently practical, the buildings were constructed using forms and materials that worked in tandem with the tropical climate. They were sited to take advantage of cooling breezes, which large, unglazed windows welcomed indoors. Deep overhangs shaded the openings from the sun, while steeply pitched roofs easily shed rain.

These are the structures that come to mind when we think of tropical living. Though humble, they are intriguing. Architecturally, they are fascinating if only because today they seem imbued with an exoticism that recalls the past, thanks to their forms and materials.

Each region also experienced a Colonial period: the Spanish and French in the Caribbean; the Dutch, English, and French in the South Pacific. At first, Europeans merely replicated their own architecture in these new places. Then, as native and foreign cultures cross-pollinated, the building of European-derived forms gradually incorporated the use of local materials. The final step in this evolution was the acceptance by Europeans of native architectural forms, which they embellished with neoclassical details. The result was the creation of the Colonial architecture tradition.

In some cases, the different European influences became intermixed as ownership of islands changed back and forth. Java, for example, was colonized by the Dutch, then taken over by the English for several years. Later, it was returned to Dutch control. As a result, some of the buildings display a salad-bowl mix of diverse styles.

This melding of influences reached beyond the island possessions themselves. The English, for instance, eagerly embraced bamboo and faux-bamboo furnishings in the Edwardian era. And the shuttered

OPPOSITE: *A soaring roof that reaches up to the sky fills this outdoor room with drama. Supported by naturalistic columns, the roof includes a small opening at the top for ventilation, allowing rising hot air to escape. The rich palette of pinks and golds is evocative of a tropical sunset.*

ABOVE: *Juxtaposing a heavily textured ceiling with the smoothness of stucco effectively communicates the essence of today's island style. A simple but elegant table assumes an almost sculptural air in the spare setting.*

streetscape and balconied buildings of New Orleans's French Quarter are lasting symbols of the French-Caribbean influence in America.

Today, modernism is the pervasive architectural influence and its effects have been felt around the world, the islands included. Many new houses and resorts in the Caribbean and South Pacific are remarkably similar to their counterparts in Dallas or Delhi. What distinguishes them is the attention to regional details, which are woven into the overall design to give these buildings a sense of place.

Ironically, the details associated with island-style architecture and design work well, though sometimes for different purposes, in climates that are far from tropical. In northern areas, steep roofs allow snow to slide easily to the ground. Shady interiors created by deep overhangs are virtually universal. And the large, breeze-funneling openings of island homes have been translated in many regions into view-framing windows that sometimes extend the width of an entire wall.

Casual in design, island-style furnishings are right at home in the informal decorating schemes often favored for sunrooms, children's rooms, screened porches, decks, and patios. They also fit seamlessly into the inherently laid-back decor of lake houses, beach cottages, and even mountain ski chalets. Offering an element of flexibility, many of these furnishings are lightweight, and hence, can be moved easily from room to room or from indoors to out. And, in many cases, the pieces are stylish, inexpensive, and durable.

It may be this blending of style, practicality, and affordability that has inspired the recent popularity of island-style design. Whether you're outfitting a vacation house in a tropical locale or decorating a home in the suburbs, island style has the power to transform your residence into a private paradise.

OPPOSITE: *Designed to achieve the light and airy look so desired today, a contemporary dining ensemble blends rattan with leather and glass. The casual look of the furnishings suits the relaxed setting, which features skylights and an abundance of plants.*

ABOVE: *As mundane a spot as a balcony railing can be an excellent place to add a bit of self-expression. Here, a balustrade of carved yellow-and-orange butterflies is capped in green. The colors—repeated in the shutters, wall, and upholstery—stand out against the background of authentic ocean blue.*

CHAPTER ONE

ISLAND SILHOUETTES

Most everyone has dreamed of escaping to a beautiful island getaway at one time or another. Envision a private retreat where rooms open to the outdoors, inviting in shady palm trees, brilliant tropical flora, and cool breezes that lull you into relaxation. With their promise of azure skies, breathtaking scenery, and a slower pace of life, the islands call to us seductively, tempting us with all they have to offer, including their architecture.

In truth, there is no single island style. Indeed, each island has its own architectural personality, the result of cultures developing in geographical isolation. Even today, the architecture reflects certain local quirks that make these water-encircled paradises distinct.

Nonetheless, it's possible to generalize. The houses built in the original manner represent what's called vernacular architecture. Known as architecture without architects, these houses were built by local inhabitants with the materials and tools at hand.

For the most part, such homes consisted of a wooden frame, supporting non-load-bearing, loosely woven bamboo walls that encouraged breezes to enter and ventilate the interior. Roofs were made of reeds, particularly on Fiji and the surrounding islands. Homes near the ocean

often stood on platforms atop stilts. This approach, still favored by builders along the Atlantic Seaboard, elevated the living quarters above flood waters. At the same time, it allowed ocean breezes to flow beneath the house, cooling it from the bottom as well as the sides.

Pre-European-influenced architecture probably reached its zenith in Bali. Early houses, raised on pilings, were framed in teak and incorporated bamboo. Later versions rested on brick or stone platforms set on the ground; they were shaded by roofs made of processed palm leaves.

Vernacular touches continue to make powerful architectural statements. The small colorful huts mounted on stilts near the bays of Jamaica immediately come to mind. In the South Pacific, many

OPPOSITE: *Although this tropical ocean view can't be duplicated, the festive island color scheme can. Basic wicker furnishings take on a refreshing new personality when painted mint green. This cool hue not only coordinates with the ceiling, but also soothes the eye. Accents of white—including the trim, posts, and Victorian-style brackets—prevent the mint hue from becoming monotonous.*

contemporary-style outbuildings such as pool houses and the like are topped by fiber roofs if for no other reason than to link the architecture of the present to the past.

The islands' Colonial era saw the introduction of European styling and materials. In the Caribbean, the English brought with them Georgian styling during the eighteenth century, Victorian in the nineteenth century. The Spanish contributed distinctive red tile roofs. In Oceania, Europeans imported the courtyard, an elegant way to promote cross-ventilation.

Gradually, the European and the indigenous merged. Incorporating influences from both, houses were constructed of local materials in vernacular shapes and embellished with European details, from classical columns to Victorian trim.

The elements of island architecture are simple, which may explain some of the appeal. As befits an equatorial or tropical setting, the majority of these elements are influenced by the climate. Starting from the top down, indigenous hipped roofs shed rain easily and add a highly distinctive and attractive look. While tile roofs immediately bring the European Colonial aesthetic to mind, many houses, both humble and high style, are now crowned with utilitarian metal to reflect the intense heat generated by the bright tropical sun and to withstand hurricane-force winds.

Despite being effective at ventilating rooms, traditional bamboo walls aren't particularly practical or secure these days. But thick Mediterranean-inspired stucco ones are, as they insulate the interior from the heat of the sun. Usually, the stucco forms an outer decorative treatment concealing cinder block construction. Though unattractive, cinder blocks offer the benefit of being insect-resistant.

Shading is no less crucial today than it was 150 years ago. That explains the continued popularity of wide overhangs that shield windows from direct sunlight. Shady verandas and pavilions remain desirable, as they enable people to comfortably enjoy the outdoors.

Even small touches such as shutters bring an island theme to mind. In Polynesia, the French popularized the shutter, which encourages air to enter and cool rooms while keeping harsh sunlight at bay. On tropical nights, shutters are flung open to maximize the flow of air. Besides working well in a range of climates, shutters are easily dusted clean. Draperies, on the other hand, often must be taken down and sent to the dry cleaner.

Climate and the availability of materials have always determined the color scheme of exteriors. Bamboo, woven palm fibers, and teak, which were used for the earliest island houses and continue to be incorporated into many new ones, create a natural look and offer interesting textures. Bright whites are in demand for reflecting heat. So, too, are pale pastels, which create the bonus of making the islands blossom into what seem like beautiful architectural bouquets.

Many elements of island style can fit into a range of environments. And if you can't pick up and move to the nearest island paradise, the next best thing is to bring a hint of the tropics to your own home.

OPPOSITE: *Europe meets the islands in a mix of white stucco, green shutters, and Palladian-inspired windows. Such elements as the columns, urns, and statuary imbue the structure with classical appeal.*

LEFT: *Tile, stone, and stucco—three of the basic building blocks of tropical architecture—unite in an inviting loggia. Terra-cotta tiles match the warmth of the exposed wood rafters overhead while providing welcome contrast to the white stucco. The tiles come to an end at the steps, where stone takes over, effectively signaling the transition between spaces.*

ABOVE: *Capable of standing up to the elements, tile is a practical flooring material for a loggia. Here, tiles in a sunbaked hue help set the island mood. Stately columns reflect the European influence, while the ceiling pays homage to indigenous island dwellings. The skylight is an unabashedly modern touch.*

ABOVE: *As if to draw attention to the hallmarks of island style, deep tropical blues highlight the shutters and louvered doors of this charming second-story porch. Pink and white join in the mix, adding a lighthearted touch that is echoed by the fanciful curlicue trim.*

OPPOSITE: *The combination of the hipped roof, dazzling white facade, and classically inspired windows gives this Jamaican house an unmistakable sense of place.*

OPPOSITE: *White stucco seems all the more brilliant when set against a turquoise sea. The effect is brought even closer to home with the addition of a sparkling pool lined in small blue tiles. A rustic wooden canopy provides shade for the poolside sitting area.*

ABOVE: *You don't have to go all out to bring a taste of the tropics to your home. Instead of focusing on the main residence, give a secondary structure, such as a pool house, a dose of island styling. This open-air design, outfitted with a bar and comfortable seating, offers welcome shade while ushering in cool breezes. A thatched roof provides the crowning touch.*

ABOVE: *During the Colonial era, Europeans translated the then-current architectural styles of the homeland into a framework suitable for island living. This Victorian-era house was "islandized" by the addition of a deep porch to shade windows; the generous proportions of the outdoor living space make it a comfortable and highly accommodating spot for relaxation.*

RIGHT: *The simplicity of this house's rectangular shape has been enlivened with generous glazing. Raised substantially above ground level and capped with a metal roof, the structure is prepared for the tropical storms that hit the islands from time to time. Thanks to its cheerful yellow and white facade, the home sports a sunny demeanor regardless of the weather.*

ABOVE: *A tile roof and white stucco walls punctuated with arches are indisputable reminders of Spain's historic presence in the Caribbean. Tested by time, these materials and motifs are as appropriate on new houses as they are on old ones.*

OPPOSITE: *A fundamental element of island living is the outdoor room. Here, exposed rafters reveal the structural "bones" of a cone-shaped ceiling that protects an outdoor living-dining room. Elevating the dining area allows it to share an unimpeded panoramic view with the living area.*

OPPOSITE and RIGHT:

Island style invades the mainland with this Santa Barbara house. A delightful pink-and-white color scheme, deep second-story porches, and a lush courtyard all bring the beauty of the tropics home.

OPPOSITE: *Natural wood finishes evoke the sultry feel of the islands. Here the earthy hue of the roof is recalled in the wicker furnishings and sisal carpeting, both of which supply intriguing textures.*

RIGHT: *Stone and fiber come together as walls and roofing for a modern house in Bali. The residence overlooks a private pool terrace where painted Chinese-style chairs and a Chippendale-inspired table reflect the enchanting color of the water.*

ABOVE: *A low, overhanging roof offers the advantage of decorating tropical outdoor spaces in an almost indoor manner. In this Balinese home, durable stone tile flooring forms a weatherproof base for elegant furnishings that don't need to be taken inside at night. Simple bamboo shades can be lowered to keep out direct sunlight, while a window shared by the adjacent living space provides ventilation.*

ABOVE: *The covered porch opens onto a shady courtyard where the focal point is a water feature. A common island motif, the water feature helps create the peaceful ambience of a quiet sanctuary.*

OPPOSITE and ABOVE: *With its lushly planted surroundings, this Balinese home offers inhabitants and guests a taste of paradise. The lower level is roofed with tile, the upper level with thatch. On the first floor, a deep veranda provides shade, forbidding entry to harsh sunlight. The lofty second level is devoted to an open-air bedroom.*

ABOVE: *The garden of a contemporary house in Bali pays homage to the island's indigenous architecture with a bamboo fence. The naturalistic privacy screen is enlivened by palms and other plants that also soften its visual impact. A large pot filled with water and lilies is a subtle tribute to the traditional garden water feature.*

RIGHT: *Stone, an important building material in Indonesia, imbues the homes of the region with a Far Eastern sensibility. This elegant material, carved and set to create pilasters and a checkerboard pattern on the floor, is paired with simple, rustic wooden columns and a fiber-clad roof.*

LEFT: *Overhangs, like the one in this Balinese home, are often designed to allow morning or early evening light to brighten verandas and other outdoor living areas while shading windows. The tile floor is impervious to water and dries quickly in the sun.*

ABOVE: *In the hands of a sensitive architect, bamboo cane ceiling supports become a riveting decorative grid. The exposed framework draws the occupant's eye overhead, not only increasing the sense of spaciousness but also providing a necessary sense of enclosure in such an open space. Bamboo appears again in both the seating and the shades for a unified look, while local pottery, produce, and flowers reinforce the sense of place.*

CHAPTER TWO
BREEZY INTERIORS

Many elements that pertain to the exteriors of island homes—materials, colors, textures, and details—extend indoors. And most of these can be adapted to environments far from the tropics. Particularly appropriate in a number of different regions are the layout of space, the approach to color, and the blending of indoors and out.

For the most part, early indigenous island houses consisted of a single room that was the setting for all family activities—eating, sleeping, and relaxing. It's easy to understand why. One-room design certainly reduced the need for materials, which had to be prepared and assembled by hand. It also shortened the time required for construction. Climate played a large role, too; the one-room house facilitated cross-ventilation. And a high ceiling allowed hot air to rise to the top of the room above the inhabitants.

A notable exception to this basic approach of constructing shelter occurred in Bali and Java. There, living spaces were often contained within a walled compound. As in the rest of the tropics, rooms were sited to take full advantage of sea breezes. This strategy naturally oriented rooms toward an ocean view, a tradition equally favored today in the design of new houses.

The homes of the wealthy in Oceania usually included a ceremonial aspect and carried highly symbolic connotations. In Bali, for example, individual buildings—which were arranged in humanlike form—functioned as freestanding wings. Bedrooms were contained in symbolic "arms"; service areas, including the kitchen, formed the "legs."

Although European colonists introduced the concept of specialized rooms to many islands where open-plan living originally dominated, the layout of residences in these regions has now come full circle. Today, as in much of the world, open-plan designs for the public areas of a home prevail. Such spaces not only offer the physical benefits previously mentioned, they also promote togetherness. In homes located in non-tropical locales, adopting an open-plan design and

OPPOSITE: *In this Balinese home, the concept of open-air design is made more practical for inclement weather with wood-framed glass doors. The cozy sleeping area seems more expansive thanks to the illusion of space created by the glazing on either side. Instead of art, the occupants have views of beautiful tropical foliage in two directions.*

incorporating a lofty cathedral ceiling can help create the backdrop for an island sensibility.

A similar evolution is evident in the windows and doors of tropical architecture. Indigenous island houses featured large openings—free of glass—to usher breezes indoors. When the European colonists arrived, however, they built their homes with smaller windows filled with glass; the glazing reflected the utilitarian function of keeping heat indoors, a goal not only unnecessary but undesirable in a tropical climate. Later houses built by Europeans took on the look of what we refer to as Colonial architecture by keeping the original European form but rendering it in local materials and with local twists such as larger windows—these being better suited to the locale.

Today, in houses located as far apart—and in such different climates—as Sioux Falls and the Solomon Islands, the trend is to open up interiors to the outdoors. Although windows sans glazing are not practical for most areas outside the tropics, a similar effect can be achieved with windowed walls and sliding glass doors. These features erase the boundaries between indoors and out, allowing the surrounding landscape to become part of everyday living.

The materials, colors, textures, and details employed in tropical houses reflect their surroundings. Many of these design elements are highly practical. The thick stucco walls that give many Caribbean homes their architectural character also insulate them from unwanted heat during the day. In Oceania, fiber walls and ceilings allow rooms to "breathe," thereby ventilating interior heat to the outdoors. Besides being durable, shaded tile floors are cool underfoot. Plus, tile stands up to water and dries easily by allowing rain from tropical storms to drain off or evaporate.

When it comes to tropical hues, the island palette is as pleasing as it is broad and versatile. It varies from room-brightening pristine white to cool, dark, saturated colors. In between are the soft pastels associated with the Caribbean and the dark, natural tones of the South Pacific.

Among the light colors favored are the ubiquitous white and coral and yellow. Trim is often rendered in dark greens and blues, reflecting the natural color scheme of the tropics. Natural, earth-tone finishes are particularly evocative of the South Pacific. While they are sometimes utilized throughout interiors, in other cases they are employed just for shutters and other accents.

Rattan, bamboo, and other local plant materials fill houses with delightful texture. Designers reinforce the visual impact of these materials with rough stone walls and tile and terrazzo floors.

Decorative architectural details fit naturally into such rooms. Some are serious and monumental, such as pediments and other classically inspired elements most frequently seen in houses from—or inspired by—the Colonial era. Others are outright fun, carved wooden banisters and the like that lighten the decorative atmosphere.

Hardly any of these decorative ideas would be out of place in year-round homes located far from the tropics. Bright whites and pale pastels work miracles at enlivening interiors in dreary northern climates. And architectural details, whether serious or fun, add interest to modern homes by engaging the eye. All that's required is a thoughtful approach, one that focuses not on re-creating the feeling of a jungle but on adding the small touches that imbue rooms with a personal sense of style.

OPPOSITE: *A coral-colored paint treatment creates a dado effect in this island-style bedroom. Although the upbeat hue is used sparingly, it is powerful enough to energize the space, which is filled with dark woods and tile.*

LEFT: *A yellow-and-white cathedral ceiling brings a lighthearted air to a stately Caribbean home. The striking treatment draws visitors' eyes upward, enhancing the spacious feeling in the otherwise simple rectangular room. For additional visual interest, the wood floor is stained in white and the white walls are juxtaposed with formal dark furnishings. A rich mahogany hue bathes the back of each bookcase, adding an extra sense of depth and picking up the tones of the wood furniture.*

RIGHT: *White envelops a British Colonial–era dining room in the Caribbean. Painted-white woodwork in the ceiling and doors blends seamlessly with stucco walls and high-gloss painted-white floors, forming a clean backdrop for dark wood furnishings that recall the days of the Empire. The high ceiling draws hot air up so that, at dining level, the room remains cool.*

LEFT: *Cream walls and pale green trim form a thoroughly pleasing combination, especially when paired with dark floors of the British Colonial tradition. A decorative arch accents the louvered doors opening onto a swimming pool.*

ABOVE: *The same soothing shade of green appears on the shutters in the living space, infusing the interior with island style.*
Although windows lacking glass—a hallmark of homes in tropical locales—are not practical in most climates, the details and color
scheme can easily take up residence anywhere.

OPPOSITE: *French doors, painted in a pastel green, are left open to take advantage of island breezes. The same refreshing tint appears on the balcony railing for a peaceful sense of continuity. Within the bedroom, a palette of white accented by delicate pastels in floral patterns creates a gardenlike setting.*

ABOVE: *Revealing the exquisite outdoor scenery, French doors transform a bath into a tranquil retreat. When privacy is desired, airy white drapes can easily be closed. A marble vanity and elegant sconces give the space a luxurious feeling.*

OPPOSITE: *In this inviting bedroom, exposed framing painted a creamy white creates an airy rustic ambience, especially when coupled with a white wooden floor that flows outdoors onto a covered terrace. A grille embellished with carvings of tropical plants enlivens the transom above the doorway.*

ABOVE: *Dark finishes on the cabinets and louvered doors create a dramatic sense of contrast in an otherwise all-white bath. Furthering the island theme are the palm fronds dangling over the doorway.*

ABOVE: *This accommodating kitchen exudes island style without sacrificing amenities. Woodwork in striking shades of blue evokes images of the sea, while the overall unfitted look gives the space a lived-in feel. Cane seating and colorful dishes enhance the tropical mood.*

RIGHT: *A wave of dark ocean blue sweeps across this cozy bathroom, creating the sensation of bathing in the sea. To brighten up the snug space, a radiant yellow ceiling shines like the sun. A mirror in a seashell-encrusted frame adds a whimsical beach touch to the decor.*

OPPOSITE: *In this sumptuous island-style room, arches and louvered doors unite to create elegant transitions between indoors and out. Tile flooring is cool to bare feet, while dark finished Colonial-inspired furnishings recall a time when the British ruled the waves.*

ABOVE: *A palette of oranges, reds, and browns imbues this bedroom with a tropical glow. Louvered doors let in air but gently filter harsh sunlight. The tile flooring has a textured look yet feels smooth and cool underfoot.*

OPPOSITE: *A lattice design graces the doors in this living area, creating mesmerizing effects on the floor as the sun's rays are filtered. The natural light that enters brightens the dark finishes of the space while allowing the interior to remain cool. Transoms illuminate the upper portion of the space, emphasizing the room's already generous proportions.*

ABOVE: *This modern interpretation of island styling embraces the outdoors with French doors and walls of windows. The design allows for efficient cross-ventilation and encourages the owners and their guests to take advantage of the deck beyond. Strong wooden beams and natural finishes enhance the island flavor.*

LEFT, TOP: *An open-plan design allows the gathering areas of this Balinese home to flow smoothly into one another. Thanks to the use of natural materials, the tremendous volume of the space is brought down to earth. The predominance of wood and the dramatic construction of the bamboo ceiling give the room an unmistakable Balinese air, which is reinforced by an array of decorative touches, including the wall hangings.*

LEFT, BOTTOM: *The open-air sitting area keeps occupants in close touch with nature. A similar effect could be achieved in a colder climate with the help of floor-to-ceiling windows and sliding glass doors. The dark finish of the wooden beams and floor is offset by white seat cushions and a natural-fiber rug.*

RIGHT: *The same materials used in the living area make their mark on the dining space for an overall sense of unity. Notice how the traditional-style ceiling, with its exposed framework, adds intriguing texture to the interior.*

OPPOSITE: *The woven walls of this Balinese bedroom would be impractical in any climate other than the tropics, but the idea can be applied to folding screens in order to create island allure in a colder locale. Similarly, the treatment at the windows could be adapted for decorative interior shutters.*

ABOVE: *With its deft mixture of wood, tile, and stone, as well as its overall palette of earthy hues, this spectacular modern bath exudes Bali style. Floor-to-ceiling glazing allows indoors and outdoors to merge, while verdant plants create a soothing scene for bathers. A garden wall ensures privacy.*

CHAPTER THREE

FURNISHINGS FOR RELAXATION

Whether your preference for furnishings veers toward the regal, the romantic, the rustic, or the just plain fun, you're bound to find the tone that you're looking for within the genre of island-style design. From casual wicker chairs and love seats to refined mahogany-stained British Colonial four-poster beds, island-style pieces can take on a number of different moods. What's more, they can make themselves at home in a variety of settings, from an everyday family room to a serene bedroom to a light-filled sunroom.

Furniture designs with their origins in the islands have been shaped by climate and culture. Historically, local craftsmen fabricated indigenous pieces with the materials at hand—rattan, wicker, and bamboo among others. Loosely woven seats and backs were designed to encourage the circulation of air, thus helping to cool the body. Similarly, beds and tables tended to be free from skirting or any other obstruction that would interfere with the flow of air.

This time-honored design line continues today. Wicker and rattan furnishings, with their light and airy designs and casual nature, are embraced for their ability to foster a sense of relaxation and comfort. From chairs, sofas, and ottomans to dining and occasional tables, there are numerous ways to introduce these materials into your decor. There are even wicker armoires in which you can store clothes or conveniently hide the television and stereo.

Many wicker pieces are available in natural finishes, much like the originals must have looked. These contribute warm, earthy tones to interiors. Other pieces are enlivened with color. While white is the perennial favorite, accentuating the breezy quality of these furnishings, tropical pastels provide a lighthearted touch.

Simple wooden furnishings also have a place in island design. These tend to be straightforward, unembellished pieces, such as slat-back chairs and square-legged tables. Many have a rustic, even primitive look.

OPPOSITE: *Wicker and rattan, hallmarks of island-style decorating, lend a casual air to a sitting area with a soaring ceiling. The delightful pineapple sign and the eye-catching aqua tint of the chairs in the foreground imbue the room with a carefree spirit.*

Some wooden chairs and sofas—both casual and more formal styles—feature caned seats, sides, and backs. This design technique, which has its origins in the islands, helps to keep the occupant comfortable by promoting the flow of air.

In recent years, British Colonial–style pieces have come of age. While some colonists brought their own European furnishings to the islands, the process of transporting these pieces by sailing ship was expensive and lengthy. As a result, many colonists settled for copies made by local craftsmen.

As one might expect, the craftsmen fabricated these pieces from the woods available. And, although they tried to make the pieces look as much as possible like the prototypes, the craftsmen understandably adapted the designs for their tools and way of working. The results were less sophisticated but nonetheless unique versions of the originals. Though purists might deride them as hopelessly provincial, the pieces possess a relaxed charm all their own.

Several years ago, furniture manufacturers began exploring this long-neglected area of design. Ultimately, the demand for pieces in this vein led them to produce entire collections of furnishings, which are now readily available.

Familiar—yet at the same time exotic—British Colonial–style furnishings possess wide appeal. Thanks to their dark wood finishes, these pieces are able to fit into a variety of design schemes, particularly those along traditional lines. What's more, their rich, dark hues pair strikingly with crisp, clean whites. Picture falling asleep every night in a four-poster bed outfitted with smooth white linens and draped in gauzy mosquito netting—another easily adaptable hallmark of island style. Such a setup is bound to inspire sweet dreams of the tropics.

A B O V E : *This enclosed porch demonstrates that island style can easily be introduced into any home. Notice how the woven seats and backs of the cane chairs pick up the subtle hues of the terrazzo tabletop. A trio of shells makes for a fitting centerpiece.*

O P P O S I T E : *A simple diamond design softened by curved insets embellishes the doors of a South Pacific–style buffet. The medium brown stain echoes the color of the floor tiles while offering contrast to the white walls.*

LEFT: *A dark wood canopy bed makes a powerful statement in an all-white room. Dressed in crisp white sheets and diaphanous netting, the inviting bed bears an air of tranquility. A lofty ceiling and an armoire with latticework detailing contribute to the room's breezy look.*

ABOVE: *A rustic farm table treated with a white wash anchors this light and airy dining area, where two Queen Anne–inspired chairs mix it up with more casual seating accented in turquoise. Framed botanical prints of island flora grace the whitewashed wall.*

OPPOSITE: *In an otherwise casual bedroom, mahogany-stained furnishings create a dignified sleeping area that recalls the Colonial era of Caribbean design. The pieces are set off against a backdrop of white walls and ocean blue louvered doors, which give the room an airy quality.*

RIGHT: *You can almost picture a wealthy Caribbean Colonial planter corresponding with customers back home in Europe at this mahogany-stained secretary. The accompanying chair with caned seat, designed for ventilation, provides a cool place to sit.*

OPPOSITE: *A caned sofa and ottoman work with a geometrically designed console to give this room a contemporary island flair. The natural-fiber floor covering reinforces the warm neutral color scheme.*

ABOVE: *Caned insets lighten the look of a dark-stained wood bed. The nightstand and blanket chest make fitting companions, thanks to their use of the same type of wood and their bold angular shapes.*

LEFT: *With its textured walls, graceful wood furnishings, and earthy hues, this bedroom has a tranquil ambience. Caning—on the chair and headboard—and a natural-fiber rug enhance the island mood. A European-style campaign desk adds an old-world touch to the eclectic yet sophisticated room.*

OPPOSITE: *On a veranda inspired by European antiquity but rendered in island materials, graceful slat-back chairs invite guests to linger in the shade as they enjoy the fresh air. A black wrought-iron table with a mosaic surface coexists in harmony with small side tables carved of native wood stained ebony.*

OPPOSITE: *Inspired by island design, a buffet manufactured on the mainland incorporates a range of tropical materials. Wicker panels add eye-catching texture at every level, while black fossil stone creates cool, smooth surfaces for resting serving pieces. A carved sunburst, indicative of the European influence, shines from below.*

ABOVE: *The minimalist approach inherent in much of Balinese design is reflected in a straightforward rectangular table and simple curved-back chairs. The contrast between the straight lines of the table and the contours of the seating creates a dynamic tension that engages the eye. The sense of simplicity is maintained by the backdrop, which features white walls, wood doors and trim, and pale stone flooring.*

LEFT: *A canopy of woven fibers tops a four-poster bed, lending the piece a naturalistic tone. The desk chair, armchair, and woven baskets further the mood. Cool green tiles grace the floor, providing a counterpoint to the warmth of the wood furnishings and accents.*

ABOVE: *An island decorating staple, humble mosquito netting reaches new heights of style rendered in lace and draped on a large four-poster bed in a Balinese home. White walls fade into the background, inviting the view of the outdoors to take center stage.*

CHAPTER FOUR

TROPICAL TOUCHES

If you want to give your home an island flair without completely outfitting it in island-style furnishings, there are plenty of decorative accents that can bring a taste of the tropics to your decor. Of course, such touches can also be used to enhance an island-style room. Not only are these accents fun to select, they are also relatively inexpensive. From window treatments and floor coverings to lamps and linens, accessories with island connotations can make a big decorative impact with a minimal financial investment. Plus, many of these accoutrements are practical as well.

Take, for example, freestanding screens. Those in the island style are made of bamboo, rattan, and other natural materials. Besides evoking the desired decorative spirit, these devices are extremely useful as room dividers. They can also hide ungainly storage or utilitarian features, such as a workstation, that might detract from the decor.

Bamboo can also be introduced into a room in the form of window treatments. Pre-cut, roll-down bamboo shades come sized to fit most common window configurations. Besides cutting unwanted glare, they help give a room an island flair. Some of the shades are made with thick bamboo cane, while others made of reed are far more refined. Colors vary, too, from dark finishes to light, natural ones.

Creating a similar effect are natural-fiber rugs. Whether made of jute, coir, or sea grass, these floor coverings contribute an earthy island texture underfoot.

Overhead, there's nothing like a ceiling fan to recall a hot tropical locale. When temperatures are soaring, these effective devices assist the air-conditioner in cooling the home. During cold weather in non-tropical regions, they can help to circulate heat, as long as you keep them on a slow speed.

Many ceiling fan models are designed to accommodate lighting fixtures. Take advantage of this design to extend an island decorating theme with appropriate shades. No ceiling fan? Then opt for other lighting options to infuse a room with a tropical attitude. Simple, even primitive, rattan shades usually will do the trick. Carry the idea further

OPPOSITE: *A low privacy screen, a bed with a woven headboard and footboard, and matchstick blinds unite to fill this room with an island flavor. Additional tropical notes are provided by the ceiling fan and the hurricane shade sheltering a pillar candle.*

by selecting a lamp base that's either in an urn shape or squared off in an Asian-style manner. Other decorative accents that are also functional include island-theme dinnerware and serving trays.

Don't overlook the potential of textiles to re-create the aura of the islands in your home. One easy step is to select a bedspread decorated with exuberant floral or palm frond patterns. Accent pillows in intense tropical colors are another means for introducing the island aesthetic into a room. Both of these strategies offer the bonus of versatility, as they can easily be changed to give your room a new look.

When it comes to decorative objects, simplicity prevails. Woven baskets in natural hues can be placed on shelves, atop ledges and tables, and in corners to infuse a room with island airs. Not only do these accessories contribute to a tropical aesthetic, but they provide handy, portable storage as well.

Ceramics introduce a sense of texture—ranging from glossy to rough—into a room. It's easy to find inexpensive yet attractive ceramic bowls and other containers for bath items. Another way to bring the island

theme indoors is with ceramic vases, which usually echo the squared-off design of lamp bases. A new item to the market is the ceramic stool, which you can find at an import specialty shop. Hollow in the center, this versatile object can double as a container for houseplants.

Framed art is yet another way to establish a zestful island mood. The least expensive approach is to place island-theme prints, drawings, oil paintings, and even textiles in rattan or bamboo frames. A variation on this idea is to use the same type of frame for a mirror above a sofa, vanity, or dresser.

Bringing the outdoors inside is an authentic way to imbue a room with an island sensibility. Seashells and other beach items such as driftwood make charming accents when lined on windowsills or mantels. Large seashells make pretty and practical containers for sponges, soaps, and other bathing necessities. Thick clusters of plants will also bring the islands to mind. Go with those that have distinct island roots, such as palms and other large-leaf varieties. With these ideas in mind, you can be well on your way to creating a functional and beautiful island decor.

ABOVE: *Island style is broad enough to include the whimsical. Here, the homeowners have selected an organically shaped chandelier with a design of flared palm fronds at its center. The small lamps are ensconced in loosely woven natural wicker shades that glow softly at night.*

OPPOSITE: *The contrast and design tension created by pairing dark furnishings and a white backdrop immediately recalls the island aesthetic. White linens contribute to this dynamic, while a large sisal area rug strikes a subtle grace note.*

LEFT: *An overhead light fixture with a wicker shade is a small but effective accent for creating an island ambience. Here, such a fixture hangs above an inlaid table surrounded by bamboo chairs in an open-plan room bathed in ocean blue.*

RIGHT: *A brilliantly colored bedspread and matching toss pillows enliven a bed frame in a sedate shade of green. The contrast is reminiscent of the unexpected color combinations found throughout the tropical islands. Draped in mosquito netting, the bed has a romantic air.*

LEFT: *Island style assumes many forms, including an almost Mediterranean look. In this Caribbean bath, tile abounds—from the large-scale terra-cotta on the floor to the far more delicate pale ceramic of the tub and walls. White walls reinforce the island sensibility and help two large mirrors reflect light throughout the room.*

ABOVE: *Earth tones for the tile and window trim bring the feeling of the beach into the bath. A bouquet of vibrantly colored tropical flowers adds an appropriate finishing touch.*

OPPOSITE: *In a minimalist bath, two large-scale seashells are the only decorative accents. They lend an organic touch to the glossy marble and glass-block surfaces while serving as convenient receptacles for soaps and sponges.*

ABOVE: *Bringing the outdoors inside is perhaps one of the easiest ways to give a room an island feeling. Here, large verdant plants in stone containers create a lush scene. For seating, the owners chose a basic garden bench in a light stain. Overhead, a skylight floods the space with sunshine.*

ABOVE: *In a room outfitted with wicker and cane furnishings, a lamp featuring a wicker base blends in effortlessly. A frock sporting a tropical print hangs on a dress form, providing a whimsical touch.*

ABOVE: *Arranged atop a vintage trunk, items with tropical associations form an evocative tableau. A carved tray, wicker glass holders, and a miniature painting of an island hut make a powerful statement when grouped together.*

LEFT: *A tall plant in a squared-off vase—a time-honored South Sea motif—reinforces the mood set by a frond-decorated bedspread. Atop the nightstand, a small woven container makes a fitting accent.*

OPPOSITE: *Quiet island touches continue throughout the room, from the natural-fiber floor covering to the ceiling fan. In between are bamboo shades and a tall palm plant. Plush cushions atop caned chairs bring a new brand of elegance to Colonial furnishings.*

LEFT: *Two statues stand watch in a richly decorated Balinese sitting room. The table is covered with a deep red cloth boasting an eye-catching border of assorted colors, including pale greens and bright yellows.*

ABOVE: *Urn-shaped lamp bases work with the caned footboard and headboard of the bed to foster an island mood. Notice how the flat-woven fiber rug recalls the texture of the caning on the bed.*

OPPOSITE: *A sensual air pervades this Balinese bedroom, thanks to a deft combination of color and texture. Lush foliage and flowers, rich red bed linens, and diaphanous mosquito netting hanging from a bamboo canopy all work together to give the space its allure.*

ABOVE: *In this peaceful setting, baskets abound, contributing natural warmth wherever they appear. Outdoors, large versions serve as practical and attractive cocktail tables. Inside, a smaller example acts as a vase.*

PHOTO CREDITS

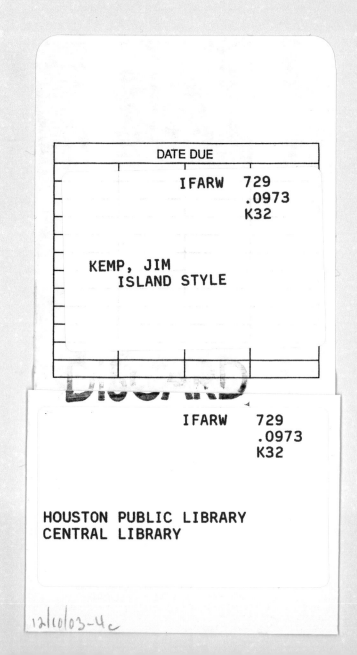
12/10/03-4c